Amazing Mai
— Book #1

THE MANIFESTATION MANIFESTO

Amazing Techniques and Strategies to Attract the Life You Want— No Visualization Required

FORBES ROBBINS BLAIR

Author of
Self-Hypnosis as You Read

Cover & Interior Design
by Rob Morrison

Copyright 2014 Forbes Robbins Blair.

4th edition: January 2017.

All rights reserved. No part of this book may be reproduced in any form or by any electronic or mechanical without permission in writing from its author, Forbes Robbins Blair

This publication is designed to provide accurate and authoritative information regarding the subject matter covered. It is sold with the understanding that the publisher is not engaged in rendering legal, accounting, psychological or other professional service. If expert assistance is required, seek the services of a competent professional person.

—From a Declaration of Principles Jointly Adopted by a Committee of the American Bar Association and a Committee of Publishers and Associations

www.forbesrobbinsblair.com

The Manifestation Manifesto / Forbes Robbins Blair — 5th edition.

1st book from the Amazing Manifestation Strategies series.

CONTENTS

CONTENTS i

INTRODUCTION - Why This Book about Manifestation? 1

Do You Manifest Like the Sorcerer's Apprentice? 2

Take Control of Your Manifestations 3

CHAPTER 1 - About Manifesting and Why It's Not Always Easy 7

Manifesting Vs. Goal Fulfillment 9

Manifesting for Lazy Daydreamers? 11

The Primary Manifesting Formula—"Future-Self Manifesting" 12

Why Manifesting Isn't Always Easy 12

CHAPTER 2 - The Mighty Subconscious: Your Key to Manifestation 15

CHAPTER 3 - How Beliefs Impact Your Ability to Manifest, and What You Can Do About It 21

How to Change a Belief 23

Five Beliefs that Notoriously Block Manifestation 24

Instantly Boost Manifestation Power with this Belief 27

CHAPTER 4 - Increase Vital Energy to Quicken Manifestation 31

Five Things that Deplete Vital Energy and How to Deal with Them 33

Nine Ways to Increase Vital Energy for Manifesting. 35

Build an Extra Amount of Vital Energy in One Minute 37

CHAPTER 5 - Emotion Control: How Feelings Impact Your Manifestations and How to Harness Them 39

Control Your Thoughts and Emotions with This Strategy 41

Five Emotions That Fuel Unfortunate Manifestations 43

Six Positive Emotions for Manifesting and How to Generate Them 45

The Technique to Generate Positive Emotions 48

Control Your Words to Control Your Manifestations 48

Stay Silent to Protect Your Manifesting Efforts 51

CHAPTER 6 - Techniques for Manifesting Without Visualizing 55

    Answer This Question to Manifest Better 56

    Why Your Vision Board Failed — and How to Fix It. 59

    The Overnight Success Manifestation Technique 62

    The Power of Pretending™ Manifestation Technique 66

CHAPTER 7 - Take the Correct Actions: What Every Lottery Winner Has in Common 69

CHAPTER 8 - The Manifestation Manifesto Meditation 73

"The Manifestation Manifesto Meditation" 77

RECOMMENDED READING 81

BOOKS+ 83

ABOUT THE AUTHOR 87

REQUEST 89

    Please Review This Book 89

NOTES 91

INTRODUCTION -

Why This Book about Manifestation?

The goal of this book is to provide ways to help you attract abundance, good fortune, a distinguished career, and happy personal relationships ... while you quit attracting painful experiences, poverty, bad luck, and contentious difficult people.

As someone who has studied the principles of manifestation since 1992, it has become clear to me that most books on this subject emphasize how to manifest bigger, better, and grander things. And, sure, we all want that. However, few books take the time to help you understand how to reduce the turmoil you attract.

For example, what good is manifesting great wealth if you also manifest illness, accidents and friends who are backstabbers?

This book is as much about how to discontinue manifesting what you don't want as it is about creating what you want.

Perhaps you've already tried to attract success by visualizing what you want, as other books recommend, but you have gotten insignificant results. This book will help.

Also, none of the techniques in this book require you to visualize anything. The results will be excellent without that.

To help your mind absorb the principles we will discuss in this book, Chapter Eight contains a life-changing narrative called The Manifestation Manifesto Meditation. And, unlike meditations in other books, you will not have to record it and play it back. The meditation will work as you read it!

Before we get into the techniques, we need to look at why your manifestation efforts and what may have gone wrong.

Do You Manifest Like the Sorcerer's Apprentice?

Perhaps you've seen the Mickey Mouse character in the Sorcerer's Apprentice from the Disney Fantasia movie. He loses control, and doesn't know how to solve his problem.

In the film, he gets hold of his master's magic hat. As he tries to use it, things go terribly wrong, because he is only an apprentice and hasn't yet learned how to properly use and direct such power. He winds up creating chaos and putting himself in danger.

Perhaps you are like Mickey—a kind of sorcerer's apprentice who has been wielding your own sort of "magic hat" your entire life—even if you didn't realize it until this moment.

Some of your manifestations have been great. And you deserve full credit for those. But some of what you've manifested probably has been messy or unfortunate or painful.

It may have happened so slowly you didn't correlate the seeds of thought you planted and the eventual garden you harvested. If this is the case for you, don't feel bad, we've all done it. This book will help to solve that.

Take Control of Your Manifestations

Your desires, your emotions, your thoughts, and your intentions are creative by nature. You cannot help but manifest your reality. You cannot help but attract people, objects, and circumstances to the orbit of your life.

You are enormously powerful.
Believe it. Accept it. Know it.
Own it. Now!

The moment you accept it, you begin to take responsibility for what you manifest—whether good or bad. And responsibility is exactly what you want. Because when you have a "take charge" attitude about what's happened in your life, you start to realize that you have more control than you once believed.

> *You realize that whatever you do, become, or acquire—it is your responsibility to manifest, and it is within your power.*

So, you see it's not a matter of whether you can manifest things. Certainly, you can.

> *The central issue is the quality of what you manifest.*

This book is not about giving you any power you do not have. You do not need any so-called "secrets." It's about providing you with the knowledge and tools to help you sort out, amplify, optimize, and direct your inherent creative manifestation abilities. It's about helping you gain more competent control so you improve the quality and beauty of what you manifest.

By implementing some of these principles, techniques, and strategies in *The Manifestation*

Manifesto you will discover how to create less chaos in your life. And you will start to generate more joy, abundance, and harmony.

CHAPTER 1 -

About Manifesting and Why It's Not Always Easy

To manifest, in the metaphysical sense, is to bring things into your life through your intention and marvelous powers of the mind.

Manifesting could take the form of concrete things like acquiring a car, a house or money. It could take the form of life-changing situations such as a new career, a healthy relationship, or the restoration of wellness.

It is said that true masters can manifest things instantly—materializing them on command. This may sound hard to believe until you consider that since we use only about ten percent of our brains, imagine what the remaining 90% might allow us to do.

If some people have discovered ways to activate some of the unused portions of the brain, is it so far-fetched to think that it might empower them to manipulate matter and energy?

However, for the substantial majority of us who are not yet masters, the process of manifesting is slower and subtler. For instance, instead of materializing some desirable object out of thin air, we attract it into our lives over time by our efforts and a series of "lucky" coincidences.

Because true masters of manifestation do not advertise themselves, they are unknown to most of us. So, the idea of manifesting is sometimes ridiculed by people who believe only in the material world and what their senses and their instruments report. They believe that mind and consciousness are the byproducts of the physical brain. Because they cannot see non-physical dimensions with their eyes or with their instruments, they conclude they don't exist. They basically believe "what you see is what you get."

Those who understand and believe in manifestation abilities and the Law of Attraction think very differently. We believe that our senses and scientific instruments are not reporting the whole story of reality.

We believe that Thought is the invisible cause of all there is, and that Thought and Mind exists independently of the brain. The brain, we contend, is a

*miraculous, living, mechanical interface
between the inner planes of Mind and
Thought and the physical world.*

Through personal experiments done in the laboratory of life, we have come to know that our thoughts can and do shape our outer lives and circumstances.

*By molding our inner world of Thought
into a more desirable one, we are
confident that the outer world will
conform to our inner changes.*

If you believe that as well, you will find the information in this book helpful and illuminating.

Manifesting Vs. Goal Fulfillment

Some people think that manifesting is the same thing as setting a goal and acting to fulfill it. While there is some overlap, they are not the same thing. Let's set the record straight.

Certainly, when we set our minds on a goal and go forth to fulfill it, we are manifesting our desire. For instance, if I have a desire for a cup of coffee and I go to Starbucks and purchase it, I have fulfilled my goal and, in a very basic sense, manifested that cup of coffee. Goal fulfillment and manifestation are not mutually exclusive.

But when we talk about manifesting, we refer to fulfilling a desire without an immediate means of fulfillment. We're talking about calling upon the powers of the mind and using the help of the Universe to bring about the object or condition we desire. Here's an example. If I had no money to purchase a cup of coffee at Starbucks, I could use my manifestation ability to fulfill my desire. The coffee might become mine in many unexpected ways or coincidences.

For instance, I might suddenly run across a coupon for a free cup of coffee at Starbucks in a newspaper. Or I might have a friend unexpectedly text and offer to treat me there. When manifestation, in this sense of the word, is at work there's no telling exactly how the means of fulfillment might show up!

To show you how goal-setting and manifestation might work together, imagine I'm getting that coffee (again) and, unexpectedly, a stranger in line offers to pay it with an act of random kindness. Here, I helped to manifest it by taking the logical action toward the fulfillment of my desire by just showing up there and letting the Universe step in to manifest it for me through that friendly stranger. This has happened to me many times. It's a fantastic way to manifest something.

Manifesting for Lazy Daydreamers?

Manifestation detractors think that people who seek to tap into those abilities feel powerless. Or they are just dreamers. Or they want something without doing the work first. Those detractors are missing the point entirely.

Manifesting is about recognizing and maximizing a faculty of the human mind to draw what we need to our lives. Why use sheer willpower and the "sweat of our brow" to fulfill our desires when we have the facility within us to get what we want faster and easier?

Self-made wealthy people often advise: "Work smarter, not harder." Which of us wants to take the long, hard path full of obstacles when we could choose a safe shortcut?

Manifesting doesn't always rule out challenging work however. It cannot give you the knowledge, skills or training you do not have. For example, say you want to become a doctor: You are going to have to go to school and train long and hard for it. No getting around that.

However, if you don't have the money to pay for that post-graduate education you could manifest the opportunities to do so.

The Primary Manifesting Formula— "Future-Self Manifesting"

The basic formula for manifesting what you want is surprisingly simple:

> *Communicate the image of your focused desire to your inner mind along with ample energy and positive emotion, and let your mind manifest that for you.*

In addition, it is widely accepted that a wonderful way to stimulate the inner mind to manifest is to visualize your desire as being part of your current reality. In other words, you would imagine that what you want is already real as you conjure the satisfaction you would feel once you've achieved it. I call it "Future-Self Manifesting."

Why Manifesting Isn't Always Easy

The formula above is sound and works remarkably well. But, as simple as it is, consistently attracting what you want is not always easy. Here are some reasons why:

1. Counterproductive beliefs. Many don't do well with the basic manifestation formula because they have beliefs and attitudes that interfere or even negate their manifestation efforts. Those beliefs must be changed so the mind and emotions are cleared from desires that block manifesting.

2. Insufficient energy. Manifesting and attracting things with the mind often requires a surplus of vital energy (aka chi, prana). When someone

performs manifestation techniques without an adequate supply of this energy, it fails to produce results.

3. Negative emotions. Emotions have tremendous power to attract circumstances to us. The failure to generate positive emotions and to eliminate negative emotions is often responsible for undesirable manifestation results.

4. Poor visualization skills. Most people are not very good at visualizing. To hold a single image in your mind without breaks in concentration is quite a mental feat. If you don't believe me, then try a simple experiment: close your eyes and picture a red apple. Notice how quickly the image changes in size, shape, color or even into something completely unrelated to an apple at all. If you are observant and honest, you will discover that clear and consistent visualization takes tremendous practice. Can it be done? Yes. But many people don't have the time or patience for it. And this is one reason they fail to produce results with the basic formula of manifestation.

5. *No action.* Some enthusiasts believe that all that is required to manifest their desires is the performance of a few techniques or meditations. Sometimes that is true. But in most cases, acting toward the manifestation goal is required.

These challenges will be addressed in this book.

CHAPTER 2 -

The Mighty Subconscious: Your Key to Manifestation

"Know Thyself" is an axiom inscribed in the outer portal at the Temple of Delphi of ancient Greece. When it comes to understanding the rules of manifestation and how they apply to you, those words carry significant importance.

All the books in the world combined would not be enough to explain who and what you are because you are wonderfully complex. But some absolute basics must be mentioned about two aspects of consciousness and how they relate to your power to manifest.

The two aspects are the Conscious mind and the Subconscious. Here is a quick overview of their functions:

1. The Conscious Mind - This is the part of the mind that directs and focuses your attention and your ability to reason. It is the part of you paying attention right now to these words as you read them. Intellect and to some extent the emotions are faculties of the conscious self.

2. The Subconscious Mind - This is the part of the mind that functions largely below the surface of your awareness. That means we are usually not aware of its activities. Yet it controls our heartbeats, digestions, and breathing. It holds your memories and behavioral patterns. And it does not sleep—ever. All your perceptions, both physical and mental, pass through it on their way to your conscious awareness.

Of these two parts of the mind, the more crucial aspect to understand is the subconscious. It is the part of you that manifests your body and your circumstances! It is also the filter or mediator for all the aspects of your mind. It is the messenger for your conscious awareness. Everything that you come to recognize consciously depends on how and what your subconscious relays to you.

The subconscious is complex, to be sure. However, how it does these things is not important. Just as you don't have to be a mechanic to drive a car, you do not need to understand how the subconscious performs its functions to get the things you want.

But there are a couple of things you should know about how the subconscious behaves so that you can formulate good strategies for manifesting what you want:

1. The subconscious is open to suggestion coming from the conscious mind. - This means you can guide your subconscious in a way that makes you happy and healthy. In fact, it's very important that you do so because the subconscious tends to follow the law of inertia: If no new directions are given to it, the subconscious will continue to follow whatever idea or pattern of behavior is already in place. When you decide that there needs to be a change in your life, your subconscious will go to work to manifest it.

2. The subconscious is what builds your body and environment. - It is what makes everything manifest. It is the real doer of the work that needs to be done. And it has access to resources of which you are consciously unaware. It remembers everything you have ever said or done, and has access to the thoughts and emotions of other people and to the Akashic records. It is very much like a magical Genie of the Lamp.

Once you submit a clear, precise suggestion to your subconscious to manifest something it immediately goes to work to accomplish it.

It takes the image and intention of what you want and harnesses its powers and storehouse of supply to bring it to you.

Therefore, you and I already have the equipment for getting what we desire. We have the Genie of the lamp at our disposal.

However, we must all learn how to carefully design what we tell our subconscious minds to do. We must present pure and non-contradictory images and intentions rather than vague or confusing ones. We must convey positive emotions to provide the subconscious with proper motivation. Because whatever we feel, our subconscious feels it too. So, if we're happy and excited about what it will feel like to find our perfect mate, to get that new job, or to go on that vacation to Italy, then our subconscious will also be happy and excited.

If we don't believe that we'll ever see Italy in person, if we think we're not smart enough to land that high-paying job, or if we feel we are not lovable enough to attract a good lover, then the subconscious will manifest those realities too!

You might say that your subconscious is extremely sensitive to your every thought, motive and feeling. It knows what you think about yourself and how you believe the world works. That's why it's necessary to evaluate and modify your thoughts, words, and feelings so you get what you want.

CHAPTER 3 -

How Beliefs Impact Your Ability to Manifest, and What You Can Do About It

In this chapter, we'll discuss the importance of your beliefs and how they impact what you manifest. I'll also provide some strategies and techniques for making those necessary changes to your belief structures.

First, what is meant by the term "beliefs"? To put it simply: beliefs are ideas, principles, and often unsubstantiated notions about things like who we are, how the world works and the meaning of Life. They are the operating systems of your mind, and they determine the quality and structures of what you manifest.

Each of us lives in our own world of beliefs. Whether we picked up our beliefs in our childhoods, from our religion, our school teachers or from our own life experiences, we base our beliefs on our preconceived limits about reality.

Our beliefs represent our perceptions of the way things are. And, just as a person's eyesight or hearing can have limitations or be impaired, our perceptions of reality can be extremely limited or impaired.

It is not my objective to tell you whether you are right or wrong about any of the assumptions you have made about your beliefs. I also don't want to tell you how to live your life. I want to call attention to how your beliefs impact what and how you manifest.

Beliefs that support and encourage you to recognize your own power and your right to wield it are beneficial and should be adopted. Beliefs that hold you back are not beneficial and should be modified or even discarded.

Look at your beliefs and consider whether they help or hinder the joyful expression of your manifestation abilities. This can be a particularly challenging task because we tend to defend our perspective of reality and ignore or rationalize the current information that contradicts it. It's the mind's way of sustaining the illusion of stability and security in an ever-changing world. While this is understandable, it can get in the way of creating the life you want.

How to Change a Belief

To change a belief, you must first challenge it. Consider taking an approach like what the author Byron Katie recommends. Ask yourself these three questions:

1. Can I know with absolute certainty that the belief is true?

2. What do I feel when I think about that belief?

3. In what ways would my life be different if I didn't believe that?

For example, there was a time when I believed I was not a good enough writer to get my work published. To challenge this belief, I asked myself if I knew for sure that my writing wasn't good enough. The answer was no because I hadn't presented my writing to anyone in the publishing industry. There was no certainty about that limiting belief about my writing.

When I thought about how I perceived my writing, it made me feel that working on my manuscript was a waste of time. It made me feel hopeless about my desire to see my work in print. It also kept me from finishing my first book.

When I asked myself how life would be different without that belief, I knew I would be excited to express myself in writing in my own way. I would be happy to have publishers and agents look at my work. I could envision people being helped by my books.

And with those positive thoughts, I began to feel empowered enough to have a brand-new sense of possibility with my writing.

Once I went through this process, I finished my first manuscript and submitted it. Within a very brief time, two publishing houses made an offer.

Ironically, the editors complimented me on the simplicity and clarity of my writing! By challenging my old belief and removing it, I cleared the way for manifesting what I wanted.

To manifest your dreams, it may take a bit of soul-searching to uncover the beliefs that may be holding you back. But it's well worth the trouble. I promise.

Five Beliefs that Notoriously Block Manifestation

Below are five common beliefs that can block your manifestation efforts. Read them and ask yourself if you believe them. After each belief, I've offered some ideas meant to challenge you as you remove each belief:

* *Blocking Belief #1: "I don't deserve to manifest what I want."* This idea is frequently attached to

feelings of guilt about having wronged people in the past. Or, it can take on a religious form of believing you are a "sinner" or you've "sinned" against God or humanity. Feeling guilty or sinful can seriously hamper your manifestation powers. One way to deal with guilt is to make amends to the person you have harmed. If that is not possible, then consider doing some charity work to "balance the scales." If you feel you have sinned, confess it to the Divine and ask for forgiveness.

* Blocking Belief #2: "Manifesting what I want means I am greedy or will become greedy." A lot of people have internalized this belief that power or money or success corrupts people. The reality is that you are already manifesting your life circumstances all the time. You are already wielding your power. Is living less successfully in any way more admirable than experiencing more success?

* Blocking Belief #3: "I must always work excessively hard to be successful." Having a healthy work ethic is a wonderful thing. There are times when we must work hard to achieve some purpose. But does that apply to life success all the time? If there were a magic machine that could manifest what you wanted automatically, wouldn't you use it instead of breaking your back to get successful?

The good news is that you do have a magic manifestation machine: It's called your subconscious mind and it can help you get what you want without excessive effort.

* Blocking Belief #4: "Other people deserve success more than I do." Some people harbor a belief that other people deserve happiness and success because they are smarter, more attractive, want it more, etc. And they tell themselves that they just don't deserve that same kind of success. But there are a lot of people who have manifested tremendous success in major areas of life who are not particularly smart or good looking or who work extremely hard for it. There are also people who have a lot of genetic or familial advantages in life but still manifest disharmony and failure.

The issue isn't whether you deserve remarkable things to happen. It's whether you are willing to allow yourself to experience joy using the manifestation powers already at your command.

* Blocking Belief #5: "Because other people are poor or miserable in this world, it is wrong for me to want to manifest an abundant life for myself." Certainly, there are a lot of impoverished people in the world. But one of the best ways to help those in need is to not be one of them. By manifesting an

abundant life, you will be able to better assist those in need.

Instantly Boost Manifestation Power with this Belief

There is a simple and virtually instantaneous way to boost your ability to start manifesting your desires right now. Here's how: Accept your ability to manifest what you want as a fact.

You may be thinking, "That's it!? What a bunch of B.S.!"

But hold on and consider this: When you are certain of any ability you have, when you know it's something you can count on to the point where you shrug your shoulders and say, "Of course I can do that," then that absolute assurance is automatically conveyed to your subconscious mind. And when that happens, your excellence at calling on that ability is virtually guaranteed, because the subconscious does exactly what you expect it to do.

The reason many people falter with their manifestation efforts is because deep down they aren't sure if they have the ability or even if those abilities exist. And if there is even the slightest doubt, it can be enough to interfere, postpone or even prevent the subconscious from using its powers favorably.

You don't need to "try hard" to use your manifestation powers.

If you do, your subconscious will behave as if your desire is difficult to manifest. The result may be a delay or cancellation of what it is you want.

The key is to have an easy confidence in your manifestation power.

Now you may be wondering, "So, how can I become confident in my manifestation powers?"

Reading manifestation books is a terrific way to get going with manifesting. Not only will you learn about it, but you will automatically generate some terrific results in your daily life. Why? Because reading and contemplating your innate abilities stimulates your subconscious mind to hasten the process.

To give you an example, prior to writing this book I decided to research the way other manifestation authors treated the subject. One book contains an anecdote about how the author manifested a cell phone charger for his car. As I read it, I remember thinking, "I could really use one of those chargers too." And I didn't think anything more about it.

A few days later, I was leaving my local gym located in a strip mall. On the pavement of the parking lot, a few paces from my car door, I matter-of-factly looked down and found a cell phone charger for a car. Talk about serendipity.

So, I picked it up and examined it, and found it was almost new and in good working condition. And since there was no way to identify who it belonged to (there were many other cars around and lots of stores in that strip mall), I felt it was surely mine to keep.

I chuckled to myself about what had happened. By just reading that manifestation author's story and immersing my mind in that subject, my own manifestation abilities were stimulated.

Lesson: If you pay close attention, you may find after reading this book, and even before you implement a single technique, things you have wanted to happen will manifest without any further effort.

This is ideal for cultivating the kind of relaxed confidence I'm talking about.

Another way to get the manifestation engine fired up is to use the power of suggestion to affirm your manifestation power. Tell yourself things like, "I attract what I want to me. I am excellent at manifesting my desires."

Performing affirmations repeatedly, in time the subconscious will eventually absorb their positive messages because it responds to repeated ideas or suggestions.

If you don't believe the truth of that, just think of how advertisers repeat their ads and commercials as often as they can. They know that by exposing the public to their services or products repeatedly more sales will result, even if they didn't have much interest in the message at the start. In fact, I've read studies that show it takes an average of seven to nine exposures to an ad for it to become effective.

Indeed, repetition persuades the subconscious to accept an idea. It works, and don't let anyone tell you otherwise. And when it works, you will discover that your manifestation efforts work faster and better giving you the confidence to make manifesting things easy.

In Chapter 8, I have an ideal way to imprint positive affirmations to your subconscious mind while you are in a relaxed condition of heightened focus.

CHAPTER 4 -

Increase Vital Energy to Quicken Manifestation

No matter what you intend to manifest, it will require the use of the subtle energy known by names such as chi, prana, mana, ruach, life force.

This living, cosmic energy is all around you. It's part of the food you eat and the air you breathe. It's in every cell of your body.

However and whenever we use our minds and bodies, we utilize this vital energy because it is the currency of life and thought. But just as some electrical appliances require more power to operate them, so certain types of thoughts require more vital energy. This is especially true when we concentrate our desires for manifesting. While very simple desires may utilize very little extra energy, larger ones often require more energy. Makes sense, right? For instance, it may take less energy to manifest a convenient parking spot in a crowded lot than it does to manifest that very expensive diamond necklace you've been admiring for months.

If you have insufficient vital energy to apply toward a desire, there can be a significant delay in its manifestation. You can still manifest it, of course, but it may require you to repeatedly submit your focused intention until enough vital force is finally supplied. It's like putting a store item on lay-away: after you have put in enough money over time, it will be yours to take home and enjoy.

It's difficult to know how the subconscious uses this vital energy to manifest desires. How it does that is not important.

The more vital energy you have at your disposal, the more energy can be used to attract what you wish to manifest.

Therefore, it is highly beneficial to do what is necessary to have a lot of vital energy available always. To have a lot of it ready for manifesting, you must acquire, replenish, and avoid unnecessary activities that deplete it.

Five Things that Deplete Vital Energy and How to Deal with Them

There are a lot of things that can deplete your vital energy. Daily living is one of them because you are using this force all the time.

However, there are some things that deplete your energy stores that may be unnecessary. By reducing or eliminating them, you can reserve your precious vital force to have more of it available for manifestation purposes.

Here are five of the most common energy drains:

1. Emotional vampires - No, we're not talking about the kind of creatures in the American television shows like True Blood or the Vampire Diaries. "Emotional vampires" are the people who drain your energy through their negative words and behaviors.

People who put you down, pull you into gossip or arguments, or who exhaust you after dealing with them are taking your vital energy from you.

It's easy to figure out who they are. After being with someone, ask yourself whether you feel tired or drained. The easiest thing to do about it is to avoid them or limit your exposure to them.

2. Anger, fear, depression - While all emotions have their place in the human experience, these emotions consume massive amounts of energy, especially if they are sustained for any significant amount of time. If you are frequently or constantly angry, fearful, or depressed, you are leaching energy. Take steps to find the source of your disposition and start to change it. Not only will you manifest better by doing that, but you'll become a lot happier. More information about emotions and manifesting is found in the next chapter.

3. Perpetual stress - Stress can certainly be a good thing at times. For example, by placing stress on our bodies through exercise, we grow stronger and healthier. But that is very different from the constant, daily stress which taxes the nervous system as it robs you of your vital force. This constant stress must be controlled or eliminated. Meditation and self-hypnosis are excellent ways to take care of perpetual stress while conserving your energy.

4. Overeating - While food can be a wonderful way to gather vital energy, eating too much food at one sitting can deplete your energy stores. That's because some of it is diverted to the digestion process. The best way to avoid this, obviously, is to eat a bit less during meals.

5. *Arguing* - It is natural to get into occasional disagreements with people in your life, but if you argue regularly you disperse your vital energy and create disharmony that often leads to undesirable manifestations. And, since most arguments are ego-based they should be avoided.

Nine Ways to Increase Vital Energy for Manifesting

There are many effortless ways to increase your vital energy. Regularly performing one or more of the following nine activities will raise your supply of vital energy:

1. Get some sun - A few minutes of direct sunlight on your face will fill you with power. While this process is automatic, it can be hastened through a simple intention that you wish to vitalize yourself with the rays of the sun.

2. Drink charged water - Place a glass pitcher of water (or tea) in direct sunlight for a couple of hours. Then drink as much as you wish. The charged water will fill you with vital energy.

3. Eat - Food contains vital energy (not to be confused with nutrition). Use the intention that you are extracting the vital energy from it. And do this every time you eat.

4. Eat foods especially full of vital energy - While all food contains some vital energy, fresh green vegetables, sushi, kelp, beef that is cooked rare or even raw (e.g. carpaccio, beef tartare) are full of vital energy. Note: Be cautious about non-cooked foods, as there are some health risks for certain people.

5. Supplement your diet - Take energy-rich supplements such as fish oil, blue-green algae, whole-food vitamins.

6. Exercise - Even a small bit of exercise goes a long way toward building your storehouse of vital energy. However, exercising to the point of exhaustion will have the reverse effect.

7. Take nature walks – For instance, as you walk through a forest you could use this phrase: "The forest is full of vital energy." That would automatically immerse you as you walk. Nature walks also have the side benefit of clearing accumulated negative junk from your magnetic field (aka your aura). For that reason, this is one of my very favorite methods to increase vital energy.

8. Meditate - By meditating just 15 to 20 minutes a day, you can greatly enhance your vital energy. It can be as simple as doing rhythmic breathing, or it could be a more complex process.

9. *Get adequate sleep* - Sleeping naturally replenishes your vital energy supply. There is no good substitute for adequate sleep.

Build an Extra Amount of Vital Energy in One Minute

Just prior to using the power of your intention to manifest a desire, it is wise and helpful to generate a surcharge of vital energy. This surcharge is supplied to the subconscious which then has all it needs to carry out the manifestation.

Here's a truly fast, easy, and surprisingly effective technique to increase vital energy that can be used for all your manifestation efforts. It was revealed to me by a Huna teacher, who said that it would also make me much more intuitive. And he was right!

This is how to do the breathing technique I recommend:

1. Draw six to ten slow, deep breaths.

2. During each inhalation, gently hold your breath. Do not puff out your cheeks or strain your lungs. Just hold each breath for several seconds, but not so long it makes you feel uncomfortable.

3. Then ... exhale slowly and smoothly.

As you do this breathing, casually and confidently recognize that you are drawing in not just air but energy, and imagine that every cell in your body is being revitalized and energized and filled with power. Imagine that millions of the tiny energy units within you are pulsing and vibrating with power and radiating light and vitality.

When you are finished with the conscious breathing, you are finished with the exercise and ready to utilize the manifestation technique of your choice.

You may also perform this exercise daily, regardless of whether you choose to implement a specific manifestation technique or not. You will then notice your increased ability to manifest the unimportant things and a boost in your intuitive faculty.

This is a simple thing, but sometimes simple techniques help us the most.

CHAPTER 5 -

Emotion Control: How Feelings Impact Your Manifestations and How to Harness Them

Many of the thoughts we have generate emotional reactions and responses within us. Some of those generated emotions may be very mild, while others may be quite strong.

Thoughts charged with strong emotion are particularly powerful at attracting things to us, for better or worse. When you think about or and feel something, that vital energy is used and vibrates on the inner plane of manifestation.

Whatever is like the quality of that vibration begins to resonate in sympathy with what you are thinking and feeling. That "sympathetic vibration" attracts those things on the inner plane. And those things eventually show up in your outer life in various forms.

They might show up as a sudden change in circumstance, good or bad "luck," opportunities or delays, good or poor health conditions, or the way other people treat you.

It is crucial that you look at and control your thoughts and emotions so you generate the vibrations to attract the things you want and repel the things you don't want.

It should be obvious that if we allow ourselves to generate negative thoughts and emotions, we will attract the negative things that resonate with them. When we produce happy thoughts and feelings, we can expect desirable circumstances to manifest for us.

Obviously, the key is to reduce the intensity and quantity of negative thoughts and feelings and to increase those beneficial ones. Being successful with this can take some work and introspection on your part.

But the goal doesn't have to be to turn you into someone who never gets upset or is always in a good mood. We are human after all, and we are going to have good and bad moments.

It's perfectly acceptable and wise to let yourself feel whatever it is you feel. Suppressing unpleasant emotions isn't the answer, because that could lead to a variety of mental and physical problems. And forcing yourself to be in a great mood when you're not is pointless and exhausting.

Instead, a more suitable goal is to notice your thoughts and emotions through Mindfulness.

> *Mindfulness is achieved by focusing your attention on the present moment, and acknowledging and accepting what you are experiencing.*

Once you become aware of our own behavior, it becomes possible to provide ourselves with some self-talk to gently control or oppose negativity and to cultivate positivity.

Control Your Thoughts and Emotions with this Strategy

One of the most helpful strategies I've found for dealing with my own thoughts and emotions is to stop directly identifying myself negatively with troubling thoughts and emotions. Instead, I take a step back and consider that my core and True Self is unflappable and calm. I do this by drawing a slow breath and silently saying to myself, "I am not my thoughts. I am not my emotions."

That way I see my thoughts and emotions as what I am experiencing rather than what defines me. After all, our thoughts and emotions are subject to change.

Thoughts and emotions are not "fixed" states. It's like being the rider of a chariot who has his horses get spooked and starts to lose control of them. The rider gets caught up in the mayhem, and starts to panic losing control of the chariot.

To regain control and manifest positive calm in his team of horses, the rider needs to quickly affirm that he is not the team of horses nor is he the chariot. He will use his reins and his calm, strong voice to calm the horses and get the chariot under control.

Like the charioteer, we can use our minds to see our thoughts, our emotions and even our bodies as vehicles (and, to some extent, as servants). When they are out of control or troubled, we can soothe, comfort, and redirect them so that they take us in the right direction—toward the life and circumstances we truly want to manifest.

As you become mindful of any negative thoughts and emotions as they happen, you can regain composure and control by repeating to yourself, "I am not these thoughts. I am not these emotions."

With a small bit of practice, you will become masterful at returning to a state of calm. And thus, you will minimize unpleasant manifestations that may result.

Five Emotions That Fuel Unfortunate Manifestations

There are several emotions that can manifest a great deal of havoc in our lives if left unchecked. Every attempt should be made to become mindful of them as they occur and to take steps to change them. Below are five emotions which can become particularly troublesome:

> *1. Self-Pity* - This may be the most insidious one. When we feel sorry for ourselves, when we have the "poor me" attitude, we carry around the thoughts that the Universe (or God, or Life) is against us and has given us an unfair deal. This victim mentality has the effect of attracting people and circumstances that confirm our belief in that victimhood. You can counter that self-pity by repeating statements like:
>
>> "The challenges of life make me stronger."
>>
>> "The Universe is on my side despite the appearance of setbacks."
>>
>> "I have a lot to feel good about myself and my life."
>
> *2. Perpetual Anger* - There are good reasons to sometimes get angry and express it. But that is very different from walking around in a state of

perpetual anger or losing your temper at the slightest inconvenience.

People who are angry all the time harbor resentment toward other people, institutions, or even to God or the Universe. This puts up a metaphorical, invisible barrier of spikes and drives people and favorable situations away from you.

You can counter that anger by repeating affirmations like:

> "I forgive all who I feel have wronged me and I return to a state of peace."
>
> "I release anger so that I may direct my energy toward manifesting happiness and love."

3. *Fear* - While fear is something that can save our lives when we sense danger, prolonged fear puts our bodies in a fight-or-flight stress response and draws to us the very thing we are afraid of. That's because we are continuously generating an image of the thing we fear. So, we inadvertently charge the image with a powerful emotion which has the unfortunate effect of manifesting that fearsome thing.

You can address fear with statements like:

> "I relax and face each day as it comes."
>
> "I handle all that comes my way with strength and intelligence."

4. Doubt - When it comes to using manifestation techniques, doubt is detrimental. It sometimes takes on the form of trying too hard to attract what you want. Those who feel the need to push their subconscious to manifest their desires get no results—or they might even attract the reverse. The best way to dissolve doubt is to learn all you can about manifestation and the law of attraction and begin with small experiments that will foster confidence in your ability to manifest.

5. Guilt - Guilt is not simply remorse. It carries with it the idea that there is a debt to be paid or a punishment because of some perceived transgression against a person or a Deity. Release this emotion by asking for forgiveness (if possible) to whomever you feel the debt is owed. If that is impossible, confess your remorse to a person in the clergy or to the Divine and perform an act of charity to make up for your transgression.

Six Positive Emotions for Manifesting and How to Generate Them

There are several emotions that are very beneficial for manifesting pleasurable conditions and circumstances. The more time you can spend generating and perpetuating these six positive emotion states, the better. Here they are:

1. *Love* - This emotion is multi-faceted and has tremendous power to attract good things and circumstances. It is essentially a feeling of care and deep consideration for someone or something. It can be deeply personal, such as love for a mate or family. Or it can take on a more transpersonal quality, such as love for humanity, nature or the Divine. Love is so powerful that it can even ease bad karma. That's one reason the Bible says that "Love covers a multitude of sins." Simply put, the more love you feel and radiate, the more love you will get back.

2. *Appreciation* - When we appreciate something, we hold it in high regard and we are grateful for our interaction with it. This can be an appreciation for a person, a favorable circumstance, or a kind deed, or even an appreciation for the beauty we notice in nature or in the world around us. This is a particularly valuable emotion for manifestation purposes.

When you imagine how your desire will appear when it comes, allow yourself to appreciate it. Not only will this help to attract what you want, but it can ensure that when it manifests, it will be everything you hoped for and bring you satisfaction.

3. *Enthusiasm* - This is an internal excitement about life or about whatever subject or object is at hand. It leads to action and is the opposite of apathy. It vibrates at a very high rate on the inner planes. It has a powerful magnetic quality that brings what we want to us quickly. Think of the last time you were excited about something, and then transfer that enthusiasm to whatever it is you are attempting to manifest.

4. *Wonder* - This emotion is the feeling of awe and curiosity about something. It can inspire and hold attention like no other emotion. That's why it is a potent emotion for manifestation purposes.

5. *Joy* - The feeling of joy often fills you with immense pleasure and makes you very happy. It can include an aspect of excitement or it can be smoothly and quietly satisfying. Either way, it vibrates at a very high rate on the inner planes and attracts abundance and naturally repels negativity.

6. *Peace* - When you feel at peace, the mind is clear of anxieties, conflict, and other negative emotions. In fact, it is an ideal state to access first so other beneficial emotions are more easily generated.

The Technique to Generate Positive Emotions

We have all felt each of the emotions mentioned above many times. You can easily generate them by sitting down for a few minutes and thinking about those times you felt positive emotions.

For instance, you might recall a situation where you felt a strong love for a person or a pet or an object. And as you remember it fully, you will notice a change in your mind and body because you will vibrate at the frequency of Love. Concentrate on this memory for several minutes. The vibration of Love will linger long after you finish this exercise.

You can use this technique daily to manifest harmonious circumstances. Or you can generate one or more of them whenever you use other manifestation techniques to provide added power.

Control Your Words to Control Your Manifestations

While it is true that our thoughts and emotions are powerful in and of themselves, when we express them aloud with words, they increase in power exponentially.

Ultimately, we should all aim to discipline our thoughts so that everything we think is in alignment with what we intend to manifest. This can take a very long time to master.

But what you can do starting right now is to begin to control the words that you speak aloud because spoken words have tremendous power to affect reality, especially those words which have negative emotion behind them. Here's how you start to control the words you use:

* When you catch yourself saying something negative with a corresponding emotion, say aloud with emotion the word: "Cancel!"

* Say it with the clear intention that you wish to preempt the manifestation that would otherwise have resulted from your emotionally charged expression. (Note: if you are in a situation in which you cannot say it aloud, then do it silently.)

There are several categories of emotionalized speech that may be responsible for manifesting disharmony in your life. The sooner you control them, the sooner you will stop the madness.

Here are the top three forms of negative speaking:

1. Complaining - When people complain about their bodies, their jobs, the government, or the weather, they are perpetuating the very experiences they are complaining about. For example, I have a friend who constantly complains about bad servers in restaurants. And whenever I am with him, sure enough, we get bad service. It's a bit humorous to watch this happen repeatedly.

He's clearly attracting this experience. Certainly, there is a time and place for making an authentic complaint, but every day-complaining muddies your magnetic field (aka your aura). The best way to counter this type of negative speech is to cultivate an attitude of gratitude and acceptance for what is. Focus on what is going right instead of what you perceive is going wrong.

2. *Gossiping* - When people gossip about others, they may not realize that the whole Universe is listening. The subconscious of the person you gossip about can hear you. Their conscious mind may not register it, but their subconscious does and this creates dissention. The manifestation can sometimes appear in the form of "bad luck." There's an old saying that applies to this: "If you don't have anything nice to say about someone then don't say anything at all."

3. *Cursing or "cussing"* - When someone uses four-letter words or uses various names for the Divine attached to negative emotion, they are creating tremendous chaos. Curse words have images attached to them. Whenever you say one, you conjure and charge the image with whatever emotion and force you put into it. While you may not manifest precisely what you've put out there, there will be an unfortunate karmic repercussion of some kind. For instance, if you call a woman the

'B' word, you may find yourself attracting women to your life who match that description. Likewise, if you use the Divine's name to condemn something and attach anger or hatred to it, you are cursing them. You will affect them with your curse whether you know it or not! When you do, there is a karmic rebound that you will experience at some point in your future, very often a severe one, such as a health impairment. So, it's wise to remove all cussing from your vocabulary immediately.

Stay Silent to Protect Your Manifesting Efforts

One of the biggest mistakes people make in their Law of Attraction and Manifestation efforts is that they fail to observe the Rule of Silence.

When you have set a manifestation goal, it is very important that you tell no one. Not me, not your law of attraction group on Facebook, not your wife or your husband. Nobody else.

*Keep your private desire
a secret from other people.*

Yes, there may be times when you need to contact or communicate with certain people who have something to do with your manifestation goals. But that's very different from walking around and telling people that you have decided to manifest something.

There are good reasons why you should keep silent about your goals. For one thing, by keeping them to yourself, you allow the energy to be more focused and intense. When you start talking to everyone about what you want and what you are going to do, you diffuse and disperse that energy.

Another reason is that never know what someone will think about your intended manifestation. On the surface, they may appear very supportive. But they might secretly want you to fail because they would be jealous if you were to succeed. Their secret desire for you to fail has manifestation power of all its own. This can seriously impede your efforts.

My best friend, for example, is a materialist. He doesn't believe in the Law of Attraction or the metaphysical concept of Manifesting. He is aware of my stance and that I am an avid practitioner of these techniques.

I have learned the hard way to never tell him anything about what I am working on when it comes to manifesting. I just don't mention it. It's completely fine with me that he doesn't believe in what I do. But if I allow him to think and talk about what I'm doing, I subject myself to disempowering suggestions from his words and the negative energy coming from his thoughts. It's better for me to just keep quiet.

This rule of silence may sound simple, but it can take some discipline to apply.

We naturally want to share our excitement about what we do and what we desire with our family and friends. But we should stop ourselves if we wish to maximize our efforts at manifesting.

CHAPTER 6 -

Techniques for Manifesting Without Visualizing

Visualization is the ability to picture something in your mind's eye. And, so many books and techniques about manifesting require the ability to visualize well. They expect you to be able to not only conjure an image in your mind of what you desire but also to keep that image constant and unchanging. The problem is for most of us this is very hard to do!

I totally agree that such a talent and skill, when combined with energy and positive emotion, produces outstanding manifestation results. But it can take years to get good at, and lifetimes to master.

While visualizing is a worthy endeavor, there are other techniques the rest of us can use to manifest what we want which work well despite our immature visualization skill sets.

The techniques in this chapter provide you with ways to make use of imagery without direct visualization.

Answer This Question to Manifest Better

Before you can begin to consciously utilize your manifestation power to any significant degree, there is a question you must answer: What do I want?

The reason that question is so important is because when you can put into words exactly what you want to manifest, the image of your desire is created in your mind even if you are unaware of it. That gives form to your intention, and your subconscious then responds to the image.

Therefore, you must determine what it is you desire to manifest. Then you must set your inner mind to that task. You might begin your statement of intention like this: *"I will use all of my powers to manifest the following desire..."*

I realize there may be a lot of things you want to manifest. And that's okay. Me too! But it's time to prioritize them and to get as clear and precise as you can. Until you do that, you will continue to receive a manifestation hodgepodge based on unfocused and sometimes contradictory commands and images you have been supplying to your subconscious mind.

Remember that you have been manifesting things your entire life. And because your beliefs, attitudes and thoughts have been charged with your emotions, your subconscious has attracted what has happened to you. As mentioned, some of it has been good; some of it has been not so good.

But now, it's time to pay attention to what you think and feel so you can manifest what you truly intend.

Pull out a notepad or your android phone right now and take a few minutes to list what you want to manifest in your life. Once you have the list, prioritize what you want to achieve in order of importance and the strength of your emotional investment. The more precise you are about what you want, the better.

Here are some examples of poor, better and great manifestation statements about manifesting money:

Poor: "I want to have a lot of money."

Better: "I desire to manifest $100,000 on or before the start of the New Year."

Great: "I will apply all of my powers to manifest workable opportunities to make a regular income of $100,000 per year or more by the start of the New Year or sooner."

Once you've written it, go down your list. One-by-one, ask yourself if you feel that it's realistic. That is, do you think it's something that you can manifest? Is it something that doesn't contradict the laws of physics, space, and time?

If the answer is no to either of those questions (if it's not realistic), scratch it off your list because it's something that isn't likely to happen.

Obviously, if something contradicts the known Laws of Nature or the Physical Universe, then it is not something your subconscious can arrange for you.

And if you feel it is too grand or outrageous or you "secretly" don't deserve, then it is not likely your subconscious will manifest it for you. That's because your subconscious knows what you think and feel. If you think something is too good to come true, then your subconscious will agree with you.

That's why those who attempt to manifest great wealth often quickly fail. They don't believe it will happen to them. Or think they don't deserve such riches.

The truth is that some people do become wealthy overnight. But if we don't think it can happen to us, then the subconscious believes that too.

While it is very possible and wise to dissolve beliefs that block your way to great or sudden success, it is also possible to establish a less grandiose intention which you find possible and feasible for you and then work your way up to the loftier manifestation goal. Start in smaller steps before tackling the biggest step.

In the case of wealth and money, this is often a better way to go. There are entire television specials dedicated to the surprisingly sad aftermaths of some of those lottery winners.

Many times, there has not been ample time to learn how to manage immense success, so the wealth is quickly scattered and lost. If, on the other hand, a person gains success slowly over time, it's more likely they will acquire the maturity to handle it wisely.

The point is that it is very possible to manifest important things in your life very quickly. If you have a clear intention in mind and you know you have the power to manifest it, then it can happen.

Sometimes, it is wiser to get to your big goals by manifesting a series of smaller, incremental desires.

Why Your Vision Board Failed — and How to Fix It

If you have read a few books or articles about the Law of Attraction or manifestation, you may have been encouraged to create a Vision Board. If you are new to the term, a Vision Board is a collage of pictures that represent the many things someone wants to manifest. It might include a picture of the car they want to drive, a vacation spot they intend to visit, or even the kind of mate they'd like to attract.

For the most part, proponents of Vision Boards instruct us to put a lot of things on the collage and look at it regularly and allow positive emotions to arise. The idea is to repeatedly expose the subconscious to these images along with a charge of emotion and that the subconscious will then go to work to materialize the "wishful dream images" on the board.

It seems like a promising idea, right? Well, many people have found that their Vision Boards haven't worked for them as promised. I made such a Vision Board back in 1992 and gave it ample time to work. I hung it in my bedroom and looked at it as often as I could while I held good thoughts. My eyes would go from image to image and I'd daydream about what it would feel like to already have my desire manifest. But after a full year of doing that on a regular basis, not one of the images/desires came true.

It wasn't until four years later, while I was studying clinical hypnosis that I figured out why my Vision Board failed. Hypnosis deals predominantly with how to communicate effectively with the subconscious. Its principles, therefore, overlap with those of manifestation techniques. Learning about hypnosis taught me a lot.

If the person being hypnotized has multiple goals, then each goal must be handled separately.

For instance, if someone wants to stop smoking and lose weight, then one session must be set up for smoking cessation and then another session must be arranged for weight loss. For hypnosis to be effective, you cannot combine both goals in one session.

That's because hypnosis allows you to focus the mind like a laser beam. But when multiple goals are introduced, this focusing power is diffused and very confusing to the subconscious.

I decided to apply what I learned to my Vision Board. But ... instead of having a collage full of different images and goals, I separated the images. Here's one example: I placed only one set of images in front of me that had to do only with the career I wanted to manifest. I looked at just those images while I allowed positive feelings to come over me.

When I was finished with this exercise, I put the images away. Days later, I placed before me the images representing my goal to get in good physical shape. Then, I allowed my positive thoughts to connect with how it would feel to be strong and fit.

Over the next few weeks, I did the same thing with the rest of the images and goals.

By concentrating on one subject area at a time, in just a few weeks I began to see all my goals manifest!

Therefore, to fix your Vision Board manifestation problem, abandon the collage concept. Instead, I suggest you create a Vision Album these five ways:

1. Obtain an empty photo album or create one on your computer.

2. On each page put images related to only one of your manifestation goals.

3. On a regular basis, pull out your photo album and look at one set of images that deal with a single subject or desire. Look at the images.

4: Connect with feelings of happiness and satisfaction or whatever you will feel once you've achieved your desire. It doesn't have to take very long at a sitting. Five to ten minutes max.

5. Put away the photo album and immediately go about your day. When you want to use your Vision Album again, you can choose to focus on any of the other images dealing with a separate goal.

Creating and using a Vision Album that separates inspiring images and goals will do what the ineffective Vision Board never could. Try it and see!

The Overnight Success Manifestation Technique

This is one of my personal favorite techniques because it is so effective and is convenient to implement.

Perhaps you have already figured out that even when you go to sleep, your mind remains very active.

Among other things, your subconscious continues to run your body and to process the thoughts and emotions of the previous day. Sleep is the perfect time to have your subconscious work on a manifestation goal, because it will be unencumbered by input coming from the conscious level of your mind.

This technique takes less than five minutes. There are just four steps:

1. Right before bedtime find an image that represents one goal you would like your mind to bring into manifestation. You can use your Vision Album, if you created one.

2. Relax as you look at the image and connect with feelings of the joy and satisfaction you will feel when your desire has already come into manifestation. Do so for five minutes or until the conjured emotions seem to fade.

3. With the gentlest of intention, affirm aloud that this is what you would to attract to your life. And know that your mind can make it so.

4. Once you've done that, go to sleep.

That's all there is to it! Overnight your mind will put things into motion to bring your desire toward manifestation.

This doesn't necessarily mean that you will get what you want the very next day. You may have to repeat the procedure many times and it may take days, weeks or longer to get what you want, depending on other factors. But rest assured, your mind will be working toward fulfilling your desire.

Because of using the Overnight Success Technique, there may be times when you have unusual or outstanding dreams. Some of them may even wake you up. If that happens, have a pad, and pen next to the bed and immediately write down your dreams. They may provide you with clues about what you can do to see your desire realized.

Similarly, when you arise in the morning please take note of any sudden flashes of insight or ideas that come to you. They may be the result of what your mind processed overnight. They may then guide you toward actions that will lead to success.

Using Imaginary Conversations to Manifest Desires

My friend Molly has been very successful in life while actively working with manifestation techniques. One day, she revealed a powerful technique she used to triple her income. I've tried it, and it has worked beautifully. It can also be used for manifestations that have nothing to do with money.

She told me that she spent time alone for a few minutes each day and on one of those days held a conversation with an imaginary friend.

In the conversation, she declared how she recently tripled her income and about how happy she was about it.

She used the past tense as if it already happened.

She would say things like, "I just got a new job and tripled my income. I'm making $90,000 now and I love what I do. It's my dream job." She told me that the imaginary conversation made it easy to feel a sense of pride and satisfaction about what it would be like to triple her income. She then imagined that her friend was astonished and very happy for her.

She kept this up over a period of weeks and landed her dream job as a national radio talk show host!

I immediately understood what makes this an outstanding manifestation technique:

* It expresses the desire aloud and with positive emotion.

* By declaring the manifestation in the past tense, it is easy to arouse the emotions of satisfaction, happiness, and appreciation.

* By repeating that same conversation over a period of days, the precise intention is reinforced.

To utilize this technique, use the following three steps:

1. Find a place where you won't be disturbed for a few minutes. You can do the technique sitting or standing.

2. Pretend there is someone in front of you and tell them that you successfully manifested what you desired. Tell them exactly what it is you manifested, and describe in detail how great it feels. Then imagine their expressions of wonder and happiness for you.

3. Perform the imaginary conversation several times a week (or every day if you wish). When you repeat it, make sure that what you want to manifest is described in the same way each time.

The Power of Pretending™ Manifestation Technique

With this technique, you set aside five to fifteen minutes during the day when you are alone so that you can imagine that what you want to manifest has already happened.

It is like the previous Imaginary Conversation Technique in many ways.

You don't need to close your eyes or attempt to visualize anything here. Instead you just pretend. Here's how to do this:

* Have a single manifestation desire in mind and then pretend it is already a fact. Think of it as though it's right now and about how your life is different.

* Consider how your life has improved and how others respond or interact to you. Let this evoke natural positive emotions, such as joy, satisfaction, and confidence.

You may choose to just sit quietly and act as if it is so and this will be adequate.

The main thing is to give your subconscious the impression that your desire is a manifested fact.

If you like, you may combine this with the Imaginary Conversation Technique as it may help you articulate and give form to your desire and tap into beneficial feelings.

You may also get creative and include props or visual aids that have something to do with the intended manifestation. For example, I used this technique to manifest a new home. Once I knew which home I wanted, I looked at the interior images of the house as a reference. I stood up and pretended to walk through each room. I pretended to walk through the front door and into the foyer. I pretended to go into the kitchen and cook myself something to eat. I pretended what the bedrooms and bathrooms were like and what it felt like to live in that house.

I wasn't sure whether I could afford the home I wanted, but circumstances came together "miraculously" so that I could manifest it!

As another example, if there is a specific car you wish to manifest, purchase a small model (e.g., a "matchbox" or toy version of it) and move it across the floor as you simultaneously pretend what it would feel like to drive it. Play and have fun with it, just as a child might. The emotion of fun is an aspect of joy. It's very powerful for attracting what you desire.

Another terrific way to use the Power of Pretending is to dress up in clothes to personify a desire you wish to manifest. You could dress up to feel wealthy or sexy.

Then stand in front of a mirror where you can see yourself dressed that way and pretend to be whatever it is you want to manifest. Have fun but be sure to take it seriously.

The image of yourself along with your positive feelings will make a very strong impression on the subconscious mind.

I have used this technique many times to tap into inner confidence, motivation, and discipline.
It is featured in my eBook/audio program:

Soul of the Knight:
Awaken the Warrior Within
(http://bit.ly/1KTS1fr)

CHAPTER 7 -

Take the Correct Actions: What Every Lottery Winner Has in Common

Want to know what action every lottery winner has in common? They acquired a ticket. In other words, they took appropriate action.

If you are a devoted reader of manifestation books and media, you have probably encountered the principle that you should not dictate to your subconscious exactly how the manifestation is to happen. For example, if you wanted to attract a romantic relationship you would not tell your subconscious precisely who you want to manifest or where and when you would meet. You would leave that up to your subconscious, because it's excellent at arranging those details.

If you consciously insist on the precise means of manifestation, you may prevent your subconscious from using its resources and interfere with the manifestation process.

This is a valid principle. However, it should not prevent you from acting toward your desire.

If you believe that you know the very next step toward manifesting your desire, take it! This communicates to your subconscious that you are serious about manifesting because your action carries with it the intention and expectation of success.

So, if you want to manifest that romantic relationship and you know what kind of person you are looking for, act and search for places where opportunities to meet someone of that caliber may be found.

If you honestly have no idea what the very next step toward the fulfillment of your desire might be, then you can leave it up to your subconscious to manifest opportunities to gain that knowledge.

In those cases, it will be up to you to pay attention to information or strange coincidences that arise in the coming days. They can show up in a variety of ways that may provide clues about what to do next.

Here are the six things to be on the lookout for:

* Books, articles, or news stories that pertain to what you want to manifest.

* Suddenly being contacted by old friends or co-workers.

* Unexpected conversations that have something directly to do with what you plan to manifest.

* New people that you happen to meet in your daily life.

* Unusual offers that might lead to the next step toward your desire.

* Dreams about how to manifest your desire.

When these kinds of things come across your path, you should act on them. Follow the trail by fulfilling several smaller tasks until you've manifested your ultimate desire.

It is true that sometimes things manifest without taking any action at all. What you want will just show up right in front of you in the form of gifts, excellent opportunities, or pure coincidence.

It's truly amazing when this happens. But this is not the only way things manifest, so it is wise to look for paths of action that reveal themselves to you and take appropriate action.

CHAPTER 8 -

The Manifestation Manifesto Meditation

I am confident that the previous chapters have provided you with a lot of useful techniques, strategies, and information to help you maximize your manifestation efforts. But I want to give you something extra powerful to move you forward quickly. That's why I am including this special chapter.

Next, you will find a remarkable meditation called "The Manifestation Manifesto Meditation." It contains affirmation statements to boost and reinforce your acceptance of your own manifestation power.

The first portion of the meditation is designed to help you achieve a condition of relaxation and heightened focus, sometimes referred to as an alpha state. This light meditative state allows your subconscious to absorb the affirmations more deeply than if you read the statements alone.

What is more remarkable about the meditation is that you do not need to record the meditation and play it back to benefit.

To get the best, fullest results simply read the meditation aloud with sincerity and emotion! It works.

In the late nineties, I discovered that it is easy to achieve a therapeutic meditative state by reading aloud a narrative designed for certain goals.

Use the Manifesto Meditation once a day for three to seven days to fully saturate your inner mind with the affirmations. Then, you can taper off and use the meditation once or twice a week or whenever you want to boost your manifestation efforts. Here's an example for when to use it: like just prior to working with any manifestation technique.

To read The Manifestation Manifesto Meditation properly, here are easy seven steps:

1. Find a place where you won't be disturbed or interrupted for fifteen minutes.

2. Sit in a chair where you can read the Manifesto Meditation clearly.

3. Read it slowly and aloud.

4. You do not read the words in parentheses aloud. They are the instructions you should follow.

5. Use a gentle, calming voice for the first part it, which is designed to relax you.

6. Use a stronger voice when you come to the Manifestation statements, and say them with emotional conviction.

7. When you finish it, sit quietly for a minute or two. Then get up, clap your hands a few times, have a drink of water and return to your everyday life.

"The Manifestation Manifesto Meditation"

"Right now, I find a quiet and comfortable space where I can easily concentrate on these words as I gently read them aloud.

"With the sound of my voice I soothe my nervous system ... calm my entire body and relax my thoughts. I speak slowly ... with a gentle but resonant tone. And as I do, I start to relax now.

"I keep my eyes open and let them blink naturally when they want to ... and they might start to feel slightly heavy and droopy ... as they would feel when I read a book before going to sleep.

"I use my imagination so that with every word I become more relaxed and drowsier.

(Imagine feeling drowsy.).

I keep my eyes open just enough to take in the following words.

"I turn my attention to my breathing, and use this opportunity to relax my mind and body more deeply.

"As I count my exhalations backwards from five to one, I let each number represent a gradually deeper level of relaxation and heightened focus.

(Draw a breath before reading each number, and count as you exhale.)

"Five ... I double my relaxation and increase my concentration.

"Four ... With every number and every breath, I relax.

"Three ... I count slowly as I meditate deeper ... deeper still.

"Two ... I use my imagination to double this meditative state.

"One ... My body is relaxed as my mind remains focused.

(Pause for five seconds and breathe normally.)

"At this level of meditation, people experience different things. Some notice interesting body sensations ... such as a warmth or tingling in their fingers. I might also have that experience.

(Pause five seconds.)

"Some people feel a floating sensation ... with a dreamy quality. I may experience that.

(Pause five seconds.)

"Whatever sensations I experience are exactly right for me at this moment. Whether I feel something unusual now or at some other time, I let that process happen on its own as I focus on the following manifesto.

"I allow my subconscious to absorb the manifesto as I read each affirmation with purpose and conviction.

(Pause for five seconds.)

"The power to manifest is fully mine, here and now.

"I acknowledge and embrace my power to manifest.

"All human beings have this power, yet I choose to use it consciously and purposefully.

"From the unlimited energy of the Universe, I attract all that I need to experience joy and abundance.

"I recognize and consider the consequences of all that I manifest. I take full responsibility.

"With awareness and intention, I apply my power for my highest good and for the welfare of others.

"All of my manifestations reflect my inner state of being. Therefore, I ever seek to grow in wisdom and to become a better person.

"With relaxed confidence, I employ the powers of Thought, Emotion and Vital Energy to manifest my desires.

"I let go of beliefs and ideas that suppress or encumber me and I cultivate those which empower me.

"I accept what I manifest with appreciation and satisfaction. I am thankful.

"I go forth with great enthusiasm with the realization that I manifest my life and circumstances.

"I am ready to take charge of my manifestations from this moment onward."

"Day by day, I grow in awareness of my power to manifest my desires with speed and accuracy."

(End of Meditation)

RECOMMENDED READING

* *Mastering Manifestation: A Practical System for Rapidly Creating Your Dream Reality* - Adam James

* *Banned Manifestation Secrets* - Richard Dotts

* *Manifesting: The Secret behind the Law of Attraction* - Alexander Janzer

* *The Secret Science Behind Miracles* - Max Freedom Long

* *The Kybalion* - Three Initiates

BOOKS+

* The Manifestation Manifesto:
Amazing Technique and Strategies to
Attract the Life You Want—
No Visualization Required

This is the first book in Forbes Robbins Blair's Amazing Manifestation Strategies series. Packed with over 20 manifestation techniques, it emphasizes how to attract what you want and repel the negativity that's holding you back. Manifesto is a perfect companion to this book. Get more about Manifesto here (amzn.to/1zsyIGi)

* The Manifestation Matrix:
Nine Steps to Manifest Money,
Success & Love

When Asking and Believing Are Not Working - This is the second book in Forbes Robbins Blair's Amazing

Manifestation Strategies series. Where Manifesto covers my approach to this subject along with practical strategies to attract what you want, Matrix goes further into ways to use practical steps to succeed. Click here to get more about Matrix: (amzn.to/1kcQoR8)

* The Genie Within: Your Wish is Granted

Based on classes Mr. Blair taught in the Baltimore-Washington DC area, this eBook and Mp3 audio course teaches you how to acquire your own Genie lamp so you can better use your imagination to manifest your wishes. It is fun, easy to do and innovative. Here's more about The Genie Within exciting law of manifestation self-improvement program: (bit.ly/1CDdH9U)

* Attract Surplus Money Mp3

Based on a script from the book More Instant Self Hypnosis, this bestselling hypnotic audio Mp3 programs your mind to attract more money to you. Soothing and effective, you can download it and listen to it right away. For more information about these hypnosis mp3s available on Forbes' site, go to his Positive Living Store: (bit.ly/1xkdNQc)

* Soul of the Knight: Awaken the Warrior Within

Tap your inner confidence, discipline, and motivation as you connect with the noble Knight within. This eBook/audio Mp3 program is like nothing else. If you are drawn to the image of medieval Knights, this program can help you transform your life quickly and dramatically. Mr. Blair believes it's the most powerful product he's ever produced. Here is more information about Soul of the Knight: (bit.ly/1KTS1fr)

* Self Hypnosis As You Read: 42 Life Changing Scripts

The newest of Forbes' self-hypnosis books, SHAYR covers scripts like "Lose the Last 10 Pounds," "Never Be Late Again," "Save More Money." These are just a few of the topics most requested by readers of Instant Self Hypnosis. This effective book contains many brand-new induction scripts and advanced material never released before. Some readers say it is Mr. Blair's best work. For more about this book, click here: (amzn.to/1uoniCk)

* Instant Self Hypnosis: How to Hypnotize Yourself with Your Eyes Open

Stop smoking, lose weight, and stop stressing out. In his original bestselling book, Forbes Robbins Blair reveals his remarkable method that allows you to hypnotize yourself as you read. It contains 35 powerful scripts to improve your life in practical ways. You'll use this book repeatedly. More information about ISH can be found here: (amzn.to/1ymUvxu)

* More Instant Self Hypnosis: Hypnotize Yourself as You Read

The sequel to Instant Self Hypnosis, this book contains 48 more self-improvement scripts covering a wide variety of topics such as "Achieve Your Potential" and "Feel More Sexy." Includes the new Master Induction 2.0. There are also new interactive experiments to help you understand self-hypnosis better and prepare you to hypnotize yourself as you read. Just read to succeed. Get more information here: (amzn.to/1ukCXNq)

ABOUT THE AUTHOR

Forbes Robbins Blair has had a lifelong interest, practitioner and professional in the subjects of self-hypnosis, metaphysics, and spirit. He is also fascinated with issues of self-determination and empowerment.

He has authored several books on these subjects including:

* The Manifestation Matrix
* The Manifestation Mindset
* The Manifestation Trilogy
* The Manifestation Revelation
* Instant Self Hypnosis
* Self Hypnosis Revolution
* More Instant Self Hypnosis
* Self Hypnosis as You Read

Since 1997, Forbes Blair maintains a personal development business (New Creations, Inc.). Its mission is to strengthen the habits of clients with tools like manifestation, self-hypnosis, law of attraction and dream symbolism.

He has produced more than 60 self-hypnosis mp3s available for instant download, which are available on his website (forbesrobbinsblair.com). The store on his site is called the Positive Living Store (bit.ly/1xkdNQc). In addition to those downloadable mp3s, he has two unique eBook-audio programs available there:

* **The Genie Within: Your Wish is Granted** (bit.ly/1CDdH9U)

* **Soul of the Knight: Awaken the Warrior Within** (bit.ly/1KTS1fr)

Visit his website here:
http://www.forbesrobbinsblair.com

Contact him by email here:
webmaster@forbesrobbinsblair.com

REQUEST

I want as many people as possible to recognize and embrace their manifestation power. It's the only way we can all take responsibility for the world we create, and make it more beautiful.

I consider it a privilege to share what I know about manifestation with my readers and clients.

You already have the power to fulfill your heart's desire. Whatever you want you can manifest.

Please Review This Book

Won't you please write a brief customer review for this book? When other people read your review, they will be inspired to join the manifestation family. Thank you.

Please review *The Manifestation Manifesto* here: (amzn.to/1kw669I)

NOTES